PRAY BY NUMBER

PRAY BY NUMBER

A DOODLE & DRAW PRAYER PRIMER FOR KIDS

SHILOH kidz

An Imprint of Barbour Publishing, Inc.

© 2020 by Barbour Publishing, Inc.

Written and created by Kelly McIntosh.

ISBN 978-1-64352-408-5

Published by Shiloh Kidz, an imprint of Barbour Publishing, 1810 Barbour Drive, Uhrichsville, Ohio 44683, www.shilohkidz.com

Our mission is to inspire the world with the life-changing message of the Bible.

Member of the
Evangelical Christian
Publishers Association

Printed in China.

000188 0420 HA

INTRODUCTION

Did you know that God wants you to talk to Him every day? Talking to God is called "praying."

When you pray to God, you can tell Him anything, because He really cares about you THAT MUCH!

It doesn't matter if it's GREAT BIG or teeny tiny. . .if it matters to you, it matters to Him!

* God wants to know when you've had a good day or a bad day.
* He wants you to tell Him about your feelings.
* If you need something, you can ask God for it.
* When you're sorry about something, you can share that with God.
* When you're thankful for something, you can tell Him that too!

Each spread in this book will guide you through a "Pray by Number" prayer.

In the space beside each number, write, draw, or doodle what you'd like to say to God. Use colored pencils or crayons to fill in each box.

Once you've completed numbers 1 through 9, use them as a guide to talk to God. And finish with number 10—by reading through a scripture selection that will help to grow your faith!

Remember, God's waiting to hear from you today!

DATE: ....

1 HI, GOD.

2 My day...

3 Something BIG...

Something *small*... 4

I'm thankful... 5

Someone needs
Your help. . .

6

I'm sorry. . .

7

I need. . .

8

9

AMEN.

10

"O Lord, hear the prayer of your servant."
NEHEMIAH 1:11

DATE:..

1 HI, GOD.

2 My day...

3 Something BIG...

Something *small*... **4**

5 I'm thankful...

6 Someone needs Your help. . .

7 I'm sorry. . .

8 I need. . .

9 AMEN.

10

The prayer from the heart. . .
right with God has much power.
JAMES 5:16

DATE: ....

1 HI, GOD.

2 My day...

3 Something BIG...

Something small... 4

I'm thankful... 5

Someone needs
Your help. . .

6

I'm sorry. . .

7

I need. . .

8

9

AMEN.

10

"My heart is happy in the Lord."
1 SAMUEL 2:1

DATE:................................

1 HI, GOD.

2 My day...

3 Something BIG...

4 Something *small*...

5 I'm thankful...

6 Someone needs Your help. . .

7 I'm sorry. . .

8 I need. . .

9 AMEN.

10

Listen to my cry for help, my King and my God.
For I pray to You.
PSALM 5:2

DATE:...

1 HI, GOD.

2 My day...

3 Something BIG...

Something *small*...

4

5 I'm thankful...

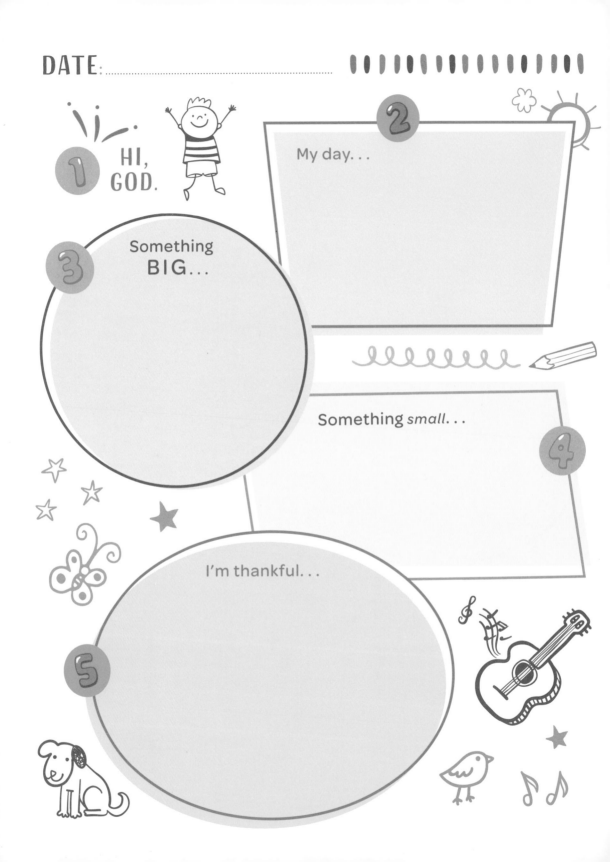

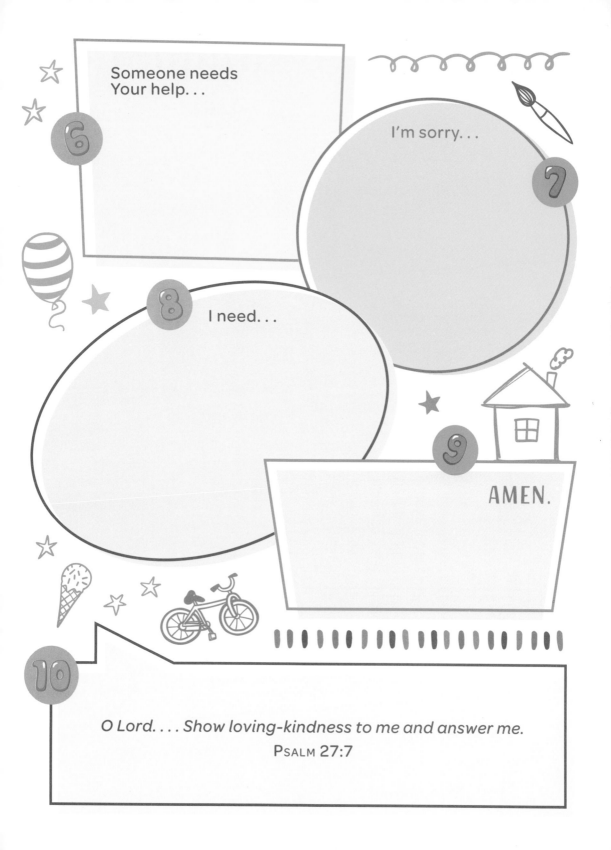

Someone needs
Your help. . .

6

I'm sorry. . .

7

8

I need. . .

9

AMEN.

10

O Lord. . . . Show loving-kindness to me and answer me.

PSALM 27:7

DATE: .... ▌▐▌▐▌▐▌▐▌▐▌▐▌▐▌▐▌▐▌

1 HI, GOD.

2 My day...

3 Something **BIG**...

4 Something *small*...

5 I'm thankful...

6 Someone needs Your help. . .

7 I'm sorry. . .

8 I need. . .

9 AMEN.

10

You must keep praying. Keep watching!
Be thankful always.
COLOSSIANS 4:2

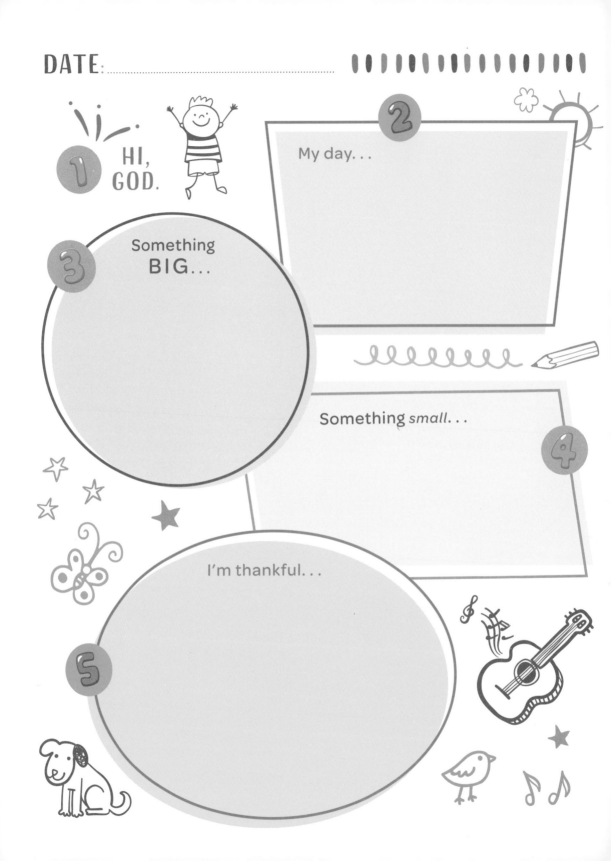

DATE:...

1 HI, GOD.

2 My day. . .

3 Something BIG. . .

4 Something *small*. . .

5 I'm thankful. . .

6 Someone needs Your help. . .

7 I'm sorry. . .

8 I need. . .

9 AMEN.

10

"O Lord, you are great and we fear You. You keep Your agreement and show loving-kindness to those who love You and keep Your Laws."

DANIEL 9:4

DATE: ....

1 HI, GOD.

2 My day...

3 Something BIG...

Something *small*...

4

I'm thankful...

5

Someone needs
Your help. . .

6

I'm sorry. . .

7

I need. . .

8

9

AMEN.

10

The Lord will send His loving-kindness in the day.
And His song will be with me in the night,
a prayer to the God of my life.
PSALM 42:8

DATE:..

1 HI, GOD.

2 My day...

3 Something BIG...

Something *small*... **4**

5 I'm thankful...

6 Someone needs Your help. . .

7 I'm sorry. . .

8 I need. . .

9 AMEN.

10 *Our hope comes from God. May He fill you with joy and peace because of your trust in Him. May your hope grow stronger by the power of the Holy Spirit.*
ROMANS 15:13

DATE:..

1 HI, GOD.

2 My day...

3 Something BIG...

Something *small*... **4**

I'm thankful... **5**

Someone needs
Your help. . .

I'm sorry. . .

I need. . .

AMEN.

"Do not stop crying to the Lord our God for us."
1 Samuel 7:8

DATE:..

1 HI, GOD.

2 My day...

3 Something BIG...

Something *small*... 4

I'm thankful... 5

6 Someone needs Your help. . .

7 I'm sorry. . .

8 I need. . .

9 AMEN.

10

We always pray and give thanks to God for you.
He is the Father of our Lord Jesus Christ.
COLOSSIANS 1:3

DATE: ....

1 HI, GOD.

2 My day...

3 Something BIG...

Something *small*... **4**

5 I'm thankful...

Someone needs
Your help...

6

I'm sorry...

7

I need...

8

AMEN.

9

First of all, I ask you to pray much for all [people]
and to give thanks for them.
1 TIMOTHY 2:1

10

DATE: ....

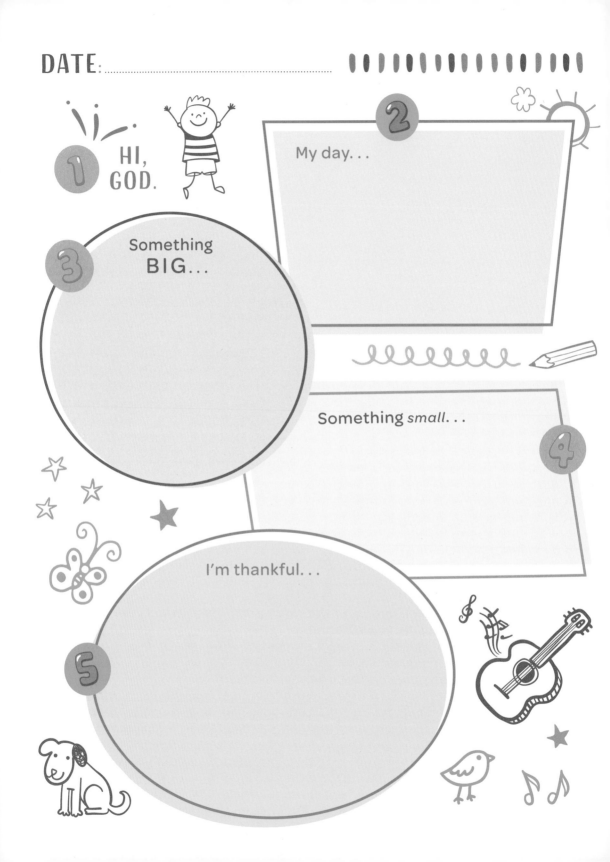

1 HI, GOD.

2 My day...

3 Something BIG...

Something *small*...

4

I'm thankful...

5

6 Someone needs Your help...

7 I'm sorry...

8 I need...

9 AMEN.

10 *Answer me, O Lord, for Your loving-kindness is good.*
PSALM 69:16

DATE: ....

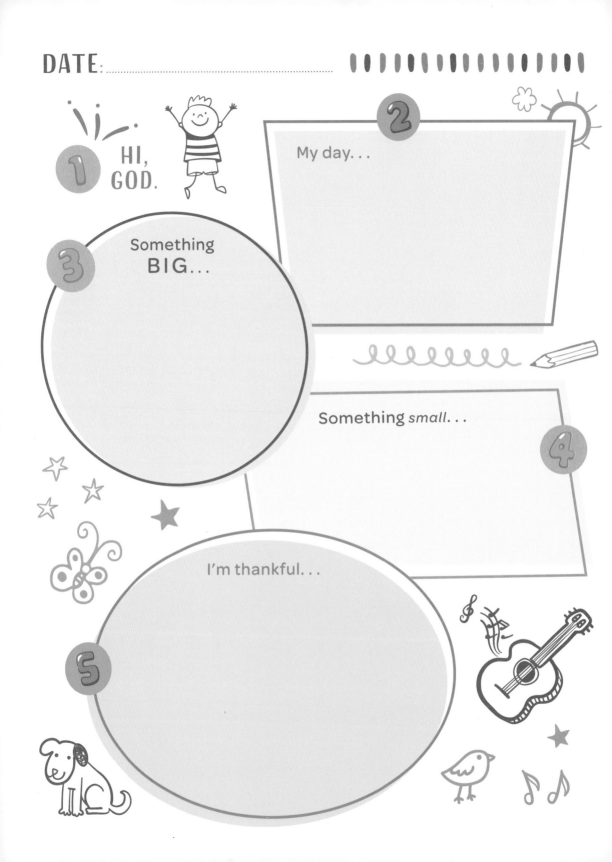

1 HI, GOD.

2 My day...

3 Something BIG...

Something *small*...

4

5 I'm thankful...

6 Someone needs Your help. . .

7 I'm sorry. . .

8 I need. . .

9 AMEN.

10

They will pray for you with great love because
God has given you His loving-favor.
2 CORINTHIANS 9:14

DATE: ....

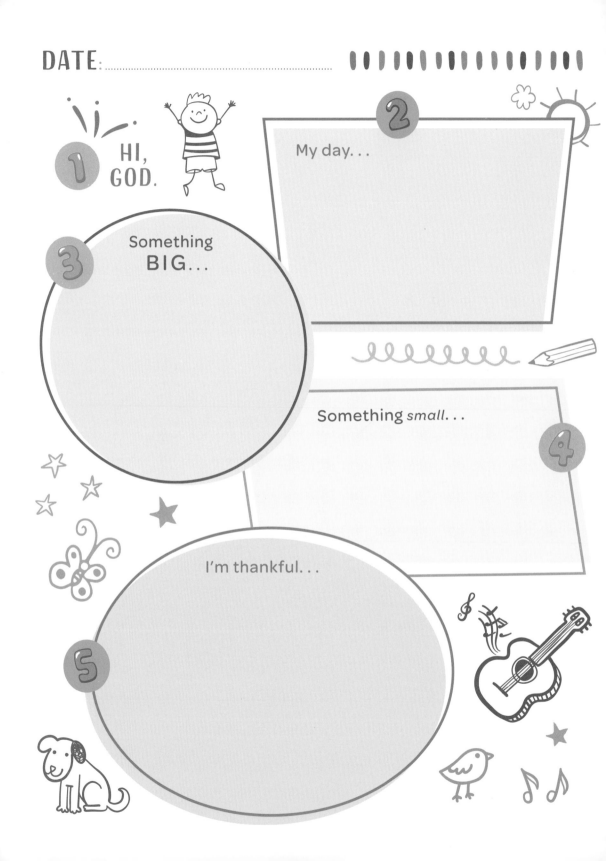

1 HI, GOD.

2 My day...

3 Something BIG...

Something *small*...

4

5 I'm thankful...

6 Someone needs Your help...

7 I'm sorry...

8 I need...

9 AMEN.

10 *I will call on Him as long as I live, because He has turned His ear to me.* PSALM 116:2

DATE: ....

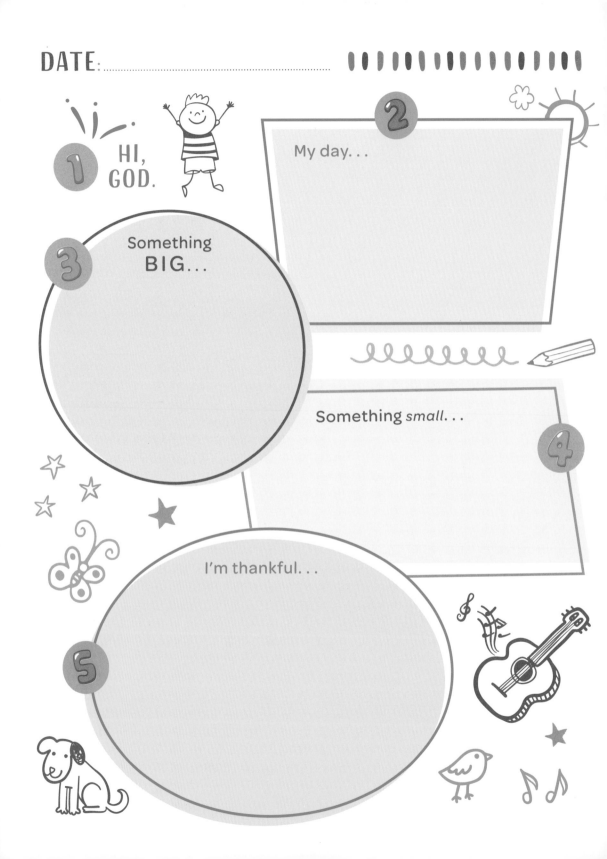

1 HI, GOD.

2 My day...

3 Something **BIG**...

Something *small*... **4**

5 I'm thankful...

6 Someone needs Your help. . .

7 I'm sorry. . .

8 I need. . .

9 AMEN.

10 *I pray that because of the riches of His shining-greatness, He will make you strong with power in your hearts through the Holy Spirit.*
EPHESIANS 3:16

DATE: ....

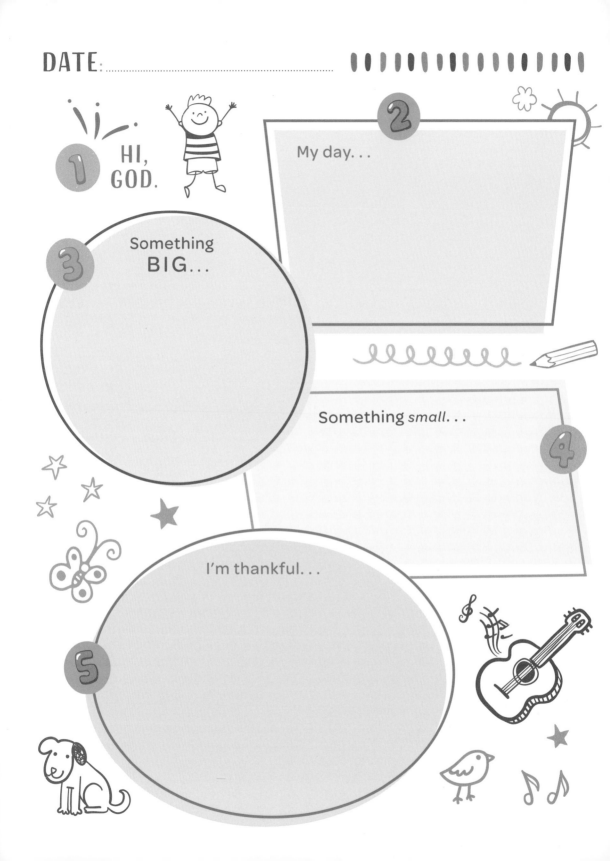

1 HI, GOD.

2 My day...

3 Something BIG...

Something *small*... **4**

5 I'm thankful...

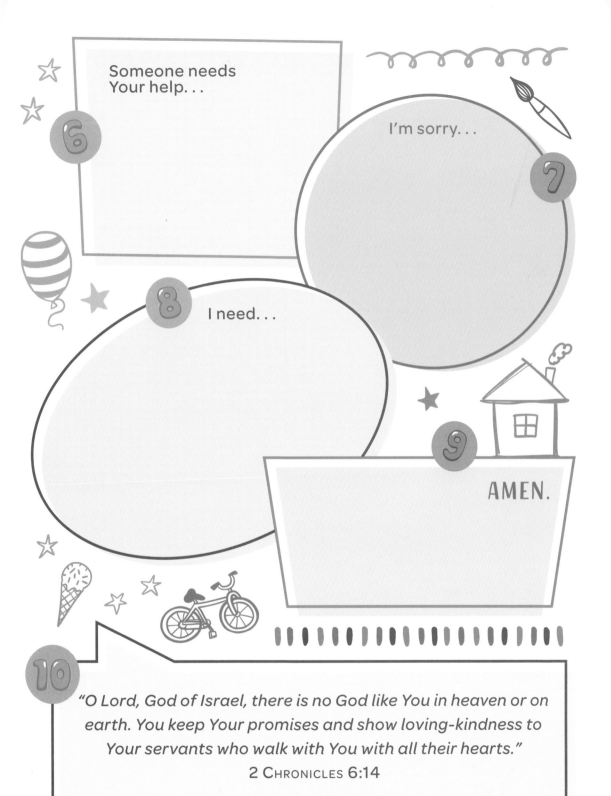

Someone needs Your help. . .

6

I'm sorry. . .

7

8

I need. . .

9

AMEN.

10

"O Lord, God of Israel, there is no God like You in heaven or on earth. You keep Your promises and show loving-kindness to Your servants who walk with You with all their hearts."

2 Chronicles 6:14

DATE: ....

1 HI, GOD.

2 My day. . .

3 Something BIG. . .

Something *small*. . . 4

I'm thankful. . .

5

Someone needs Your help. . .

6

I'm sorry. . .

7

8

I need. . .

9

AMEN.

10

The Good News tells us we are made right with God by faith in Him. Then, by faith we live that new life through Him.
ROMANS 1:17

DATE: ....

1 HI, GOD.

2 My day...

3 Something BIG...

4 Something *small*...

5 I'm thankful...

Someone needs Your help. . .

6

I'm sorry. . .

7

8

I need. . .

9

AMEN.

10

I put out my hands to You. My soul is thirsty for You like a dry land.
PSALM 143:6

DATE: ....

1 HI, GOD.

2 My day...

3 Something BIG...

Something *small*... 4

I'm thankful...

5

6 Someone needs
Your help...

7 I'm sorry...

8 I need...

9 AMEN.

10 *"Respect and give thanks for those who try to bring bad to you. Pray for those who make it very hard for you."*
LUKE 6:28

DATE:...

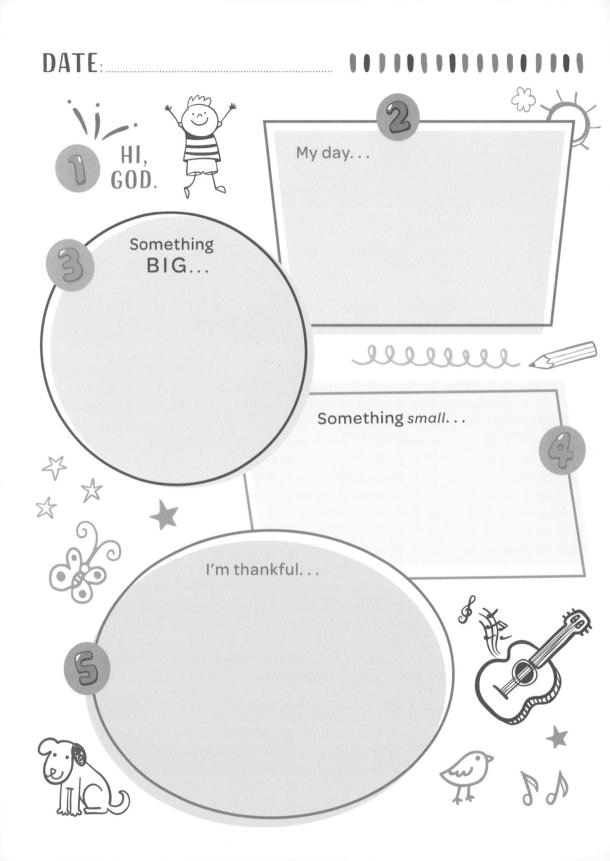

1 HI, GOD.

2 My day...

3 Something BIG...

Something *small*... **4**

5 I'm thankful...

6 Someone needs Your help. . .

7 I'm sorry. . .

8 I need. . .

9 AMEN.

10 *I pray that your love will grow more and more. I pray that you will have better understanding and be wise in all things.*
PHILIPPIANS 1:9

DATE:..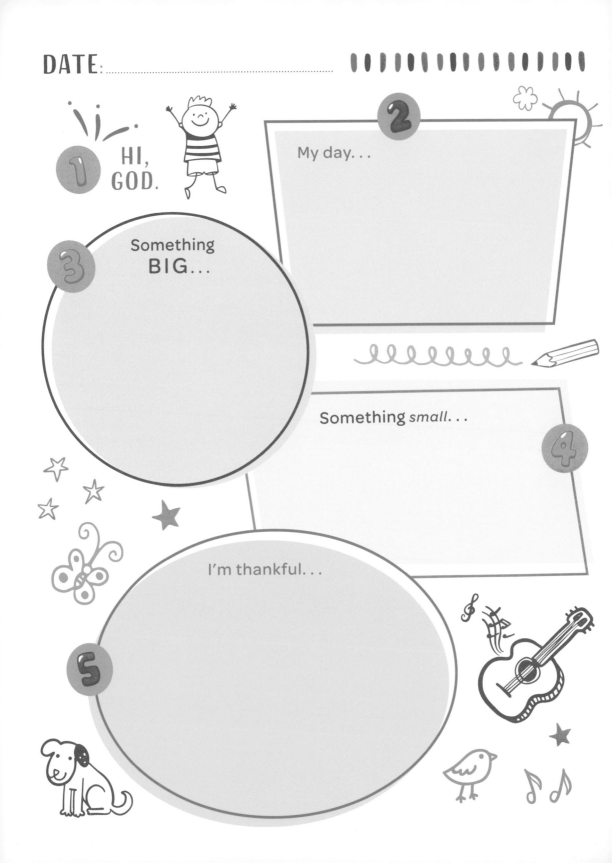

1 HI, GOD.

2 My day...

3 Something BIG...

Something *small*... **4**

5 I'm thankful...

6 Someone needs Your help. . .

7 I'm sorry. . .

8 I need. . .

9 AMEN.

10 *"But I tell you, love those who hate you. . . .*
Pray for those who do bad things to you."
MATTHEW 5:44

DATE: ....

1 HI, GOD.

2 My day...

3 Something **BIG**...

Something *small*... **4**

5 I'm thankful...

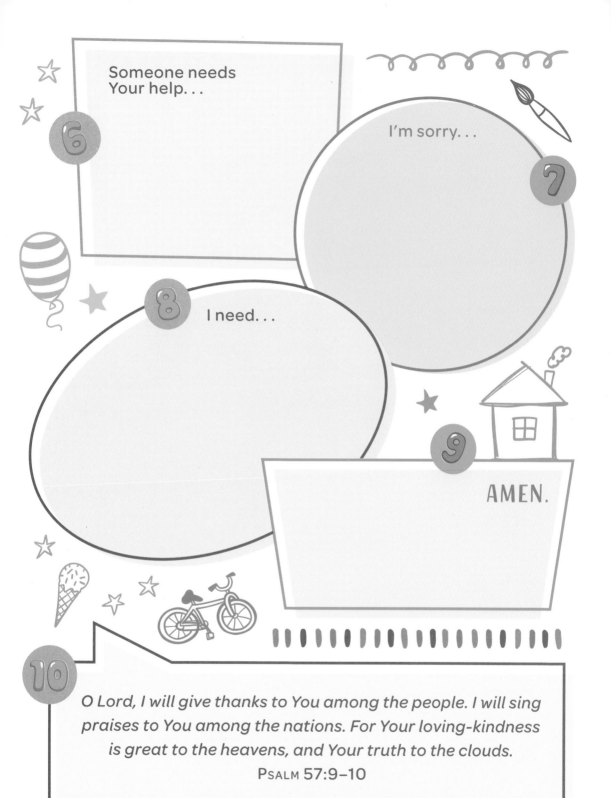

Someone needs Your help. . .

6

I'm sorry. . .

7

I need. . .

8

9

AMEN.

10

O Lord, I will give thanks to You among the people. I will sing praises to You among the nations. For Your loving-kindness is great to the heavens, and Your truth to the clouds.

Psalm 57:9–10

DATE:

1 HI, GOD.

2 My day. . .

3 Something BIG. . .

4 Something *small*. . .

5 I'm thankful. . .

6 Someone needs Your help. . .

7 I'm sorry. . .

8 I need. . .

9 AMEN.

10

O Lord, to You I call. O my Rock, listen to me.
PSALM 28:1

DATE: .... |||||||||||||||||||

1 HI, GOD.

2 My day...

3 Something **BIG**...

Something *small*... **4**

I'm thankful... **5**

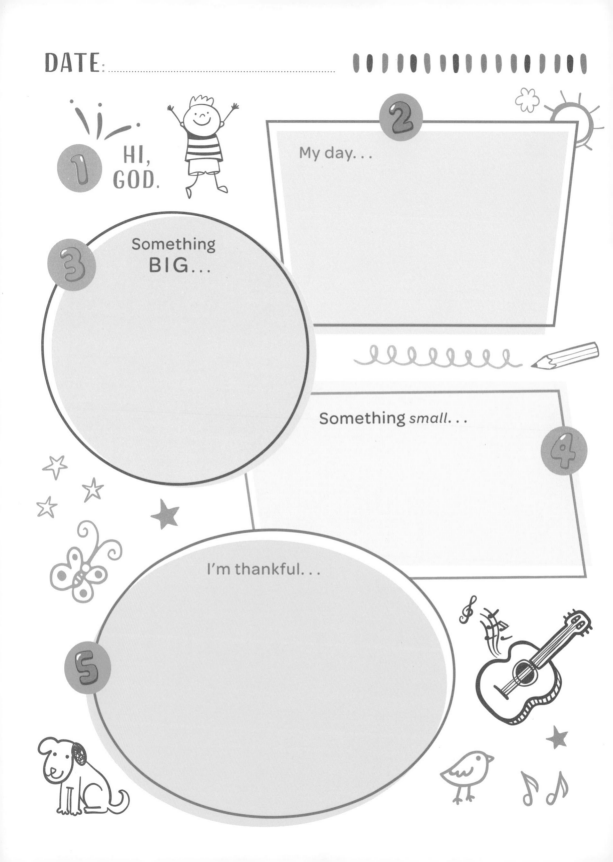

Someone needs
Your help. . .

6

I'm sorry. . .

7

8

I need. . .

9

AMEN.

10

*I pray that you will know how great His power is
for those who have put their trust in Him.*
EPHESIANS 1:19

DATE: ....

1 HI, GOD.

2 My day...

3 Something BIG...

Something *small*... 4

I'm thankful... 5

Someone needs Your help. . .

6

I'm sorry. . .

7

8

I need. . .

9

AMEN.

10

"All things you ask for in prayer,
you will receive if you have faith."
MATTHEW 21:22

DATE:..

1 HI, GOD.

2 My day...

3 Something BIG...

Something *small*...

4

5 I'm thankful...

6 Someone needs
Your help...

7 I'm sorry...

8 I need...

9 AMEN.

10

Answer me with Your saving truth in Your
great loving-kindness, O God.
PSALM 69:13

DATE:..

1 HI, GOD.

2 My day...

3 Something BIG...

Something *small*... 4

5 I'm thankful...

Someone needs Your help...

6

I'm sorry...

7

8   I need...

9

AMEN.

10

But as for me, it is good to be near God. I have made the Lord God my safe place. So I may tell of all the things You have done.
PSALM 73:28

DATE:..

1 HI, GOD.

2 My day...

3 Something BIG...

4 Something *small*...

5 I'm thankful...

Someone needs Your help. . .

6

I'm sorry. . .

7

8

I need. . .

9

AMEN.

10

Then [Jesus] went away by Himself to pray in a desert.
LUKE 5:16

DATE: ....

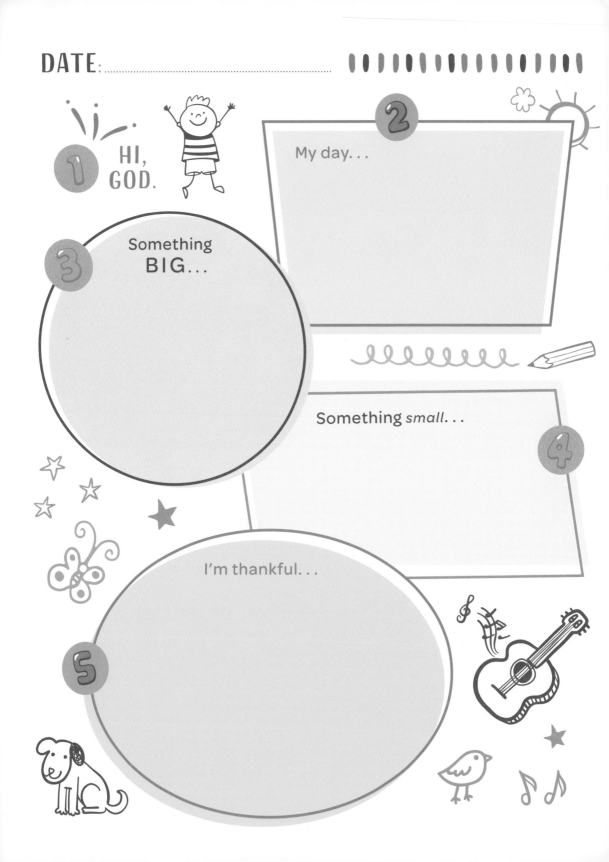

1 HI, GOD.

2 My day...

3 Something BIG...

Something *small*... **4**

5 I'm thankful...

6 Someone needs
Your help. . .

7 I'm sorry. . .

8 I need. . .

9 AMEN.

10 *I will sing of the loving-kindness of the Lord forever.*
I will make known with my mouth how
faithful You are to all people.
PSALM 89:1

DATE:...................................

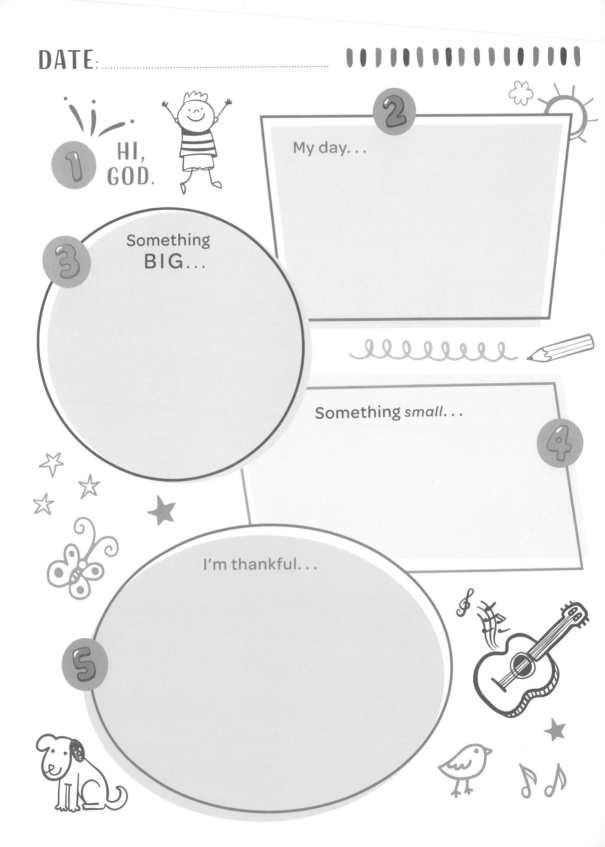

1 HI, GOD.

2 My day...

3 Something BIG...

Something *small*...

4

5 I'm thankful...

Someone needs
Your help...

6

I'm sorry...

7

8

I need...

9

AMEN.

10

*Honor and thanks be to God! He has not turned away from
my prayer or held His loving-kindness from me.*
PSALM 66:20

DATE: ....

1 HI, GOD.

2 My day...

3 Something BIG...

Something *small*...

4

5 I'm thankful...

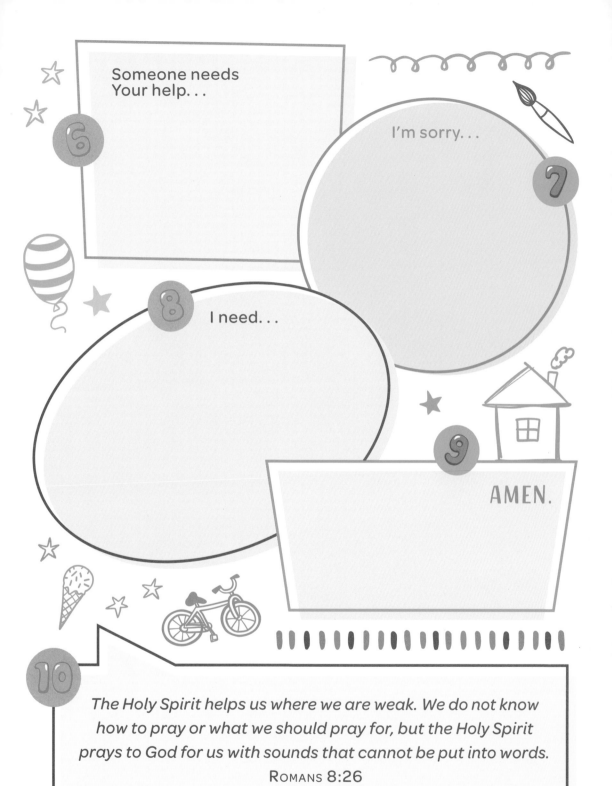

Someone needs
Your help...

6

I'm sorry...

7

8

I need...

9

AMEN.

10

*The Holy Spirit helps us where we are weak. We do not know
how to pray or what we should pray for, but the Holy Spirit
prays to God for us with sounds that cannot be put into words.*
ROMANS 8:26

DATE:

1 HI, GOD.

2 My day...

3 Something BIG...

Something *small*...

4

5 I'm thankful...

Someone needs Your help. . .

6

I'm sorry. . .

7

8 **I need. . .**

9

AMEN.

10

Be happy in your hope. Do not give up when trouble comes. Do not let anything stop you from praying.
ROMANS 12:12

DATE: ....

1 HI, GOD.

2 My day...

3 Something BIG...

Something *small*...

4

5 I'm thankful...

6 Someone needs Your help. . .

7 I'm sorry. . .

8 I need. . .

9 AMEN.

10

So my soul may sing praise to You, and not be quiet.
O Lord my God, I will give thanks to You forever.
Psalm **30:12**

DATE: ....

1 HI, GOD.

2 My day...

3 Something BIG...

Something *small*... **4**

5 I'm thankful...

6 Someone needs Your help. . .

7 I'm sorry. . .

8 I need. . .

9 AMEN.

10

I have called to You, O God, for You will answer me.
Listen to me and hear my words.
PSALM 17:6

DATE: ....

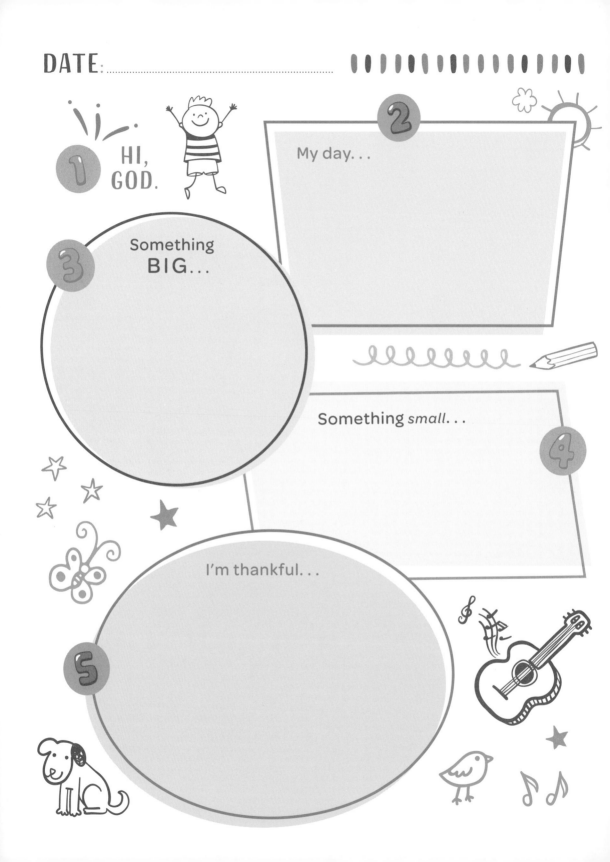

1 HI, GOD.

2 My day...

3 Something BIG...

Something *small*... **4**

5 I'm thankful...

6 Someone needs Your help. . .

7 I'm sorry. . .

8 I need. . .

9 AMEN.

10 *You also help us by praying for us. Many people thank God for His favor to us. This is an answer to the prayers of many people.*
2 Corinthians 1:11

DATE:...

1 HI, GOD.

2 My day...

3 Something BIG...

Something *small...* **4**

5 I'm thankful...

6 Someone needs Your help. . .

7 I'm sorry. . .

8 I need. . .

9 AMEN.

10

I love the Lord, because He hears my voice and my prayers.
PSALM 116:1

DATE: .... |||||||||||||||||||

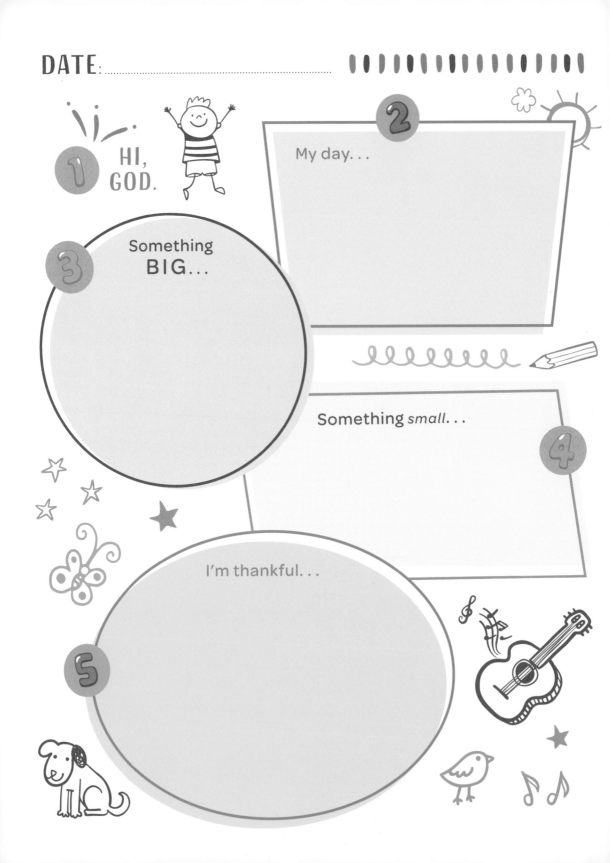

1 HI, GOD.

2 My day...

3 Something **BIG**...

Something *small*... **4**

I'm thankful... **5**

6 Someone needs Your help...

7 I'm sorry...

8 I need...

9 AMEN.

10

I always give thanks for you and pray for you.
Ephesians 1:16

DATE:..

1 HI, GOD.

2 My day...

3 Something BIG...

Something *small...* **4**

5 I'm thankful...

Someone needs
Your help. . .

6

I'm sorry. . .

7

I need. . .

8

9

AMEN.

10

*The Lord is my strength and my safe cover.
My heart trusts in Him, and I am helped. So my
heart is full of joy. I will thank Him with my song.*
PSALM 28:7

DATE:...

1 HI, GOD.

2 My day...

3 Something BIG...

Something small... 4

5 I'm thankful...

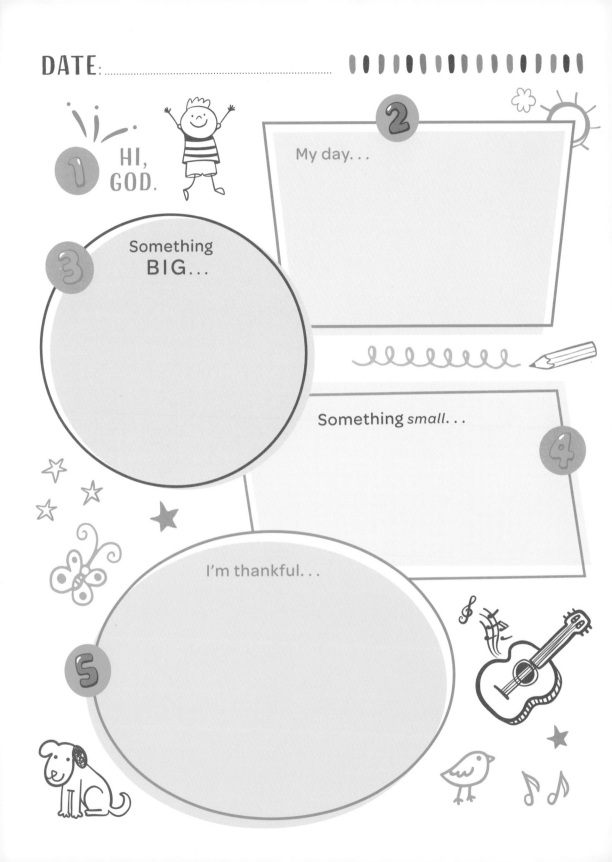

6 Someone needs Your help. . .

7 I'm sorry. . .

8 I need. . .

9 AMEN.

10 *I will give You thanks forever because of what You have done. And I will hope in Your name, for it is good to be where those who belong to You are.*

Psalm 52:9

DATE:...

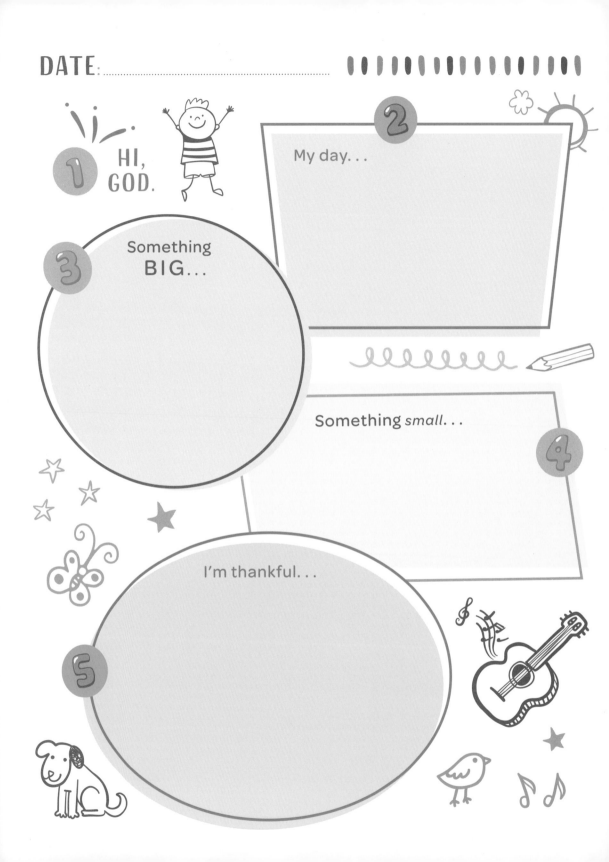

1 HI, GOD.

2 My day...

3 Something BIG...

Something *small*... **4**

I'm thankful... **5**

Someone needs Your help. . .

6

I'm sorry. . .

7

I need. . .

8

9

AMEN.

10

O God Who saves us, You answer us in the way that is right and good by Your great works that make people stand in fear. You are the hope of all the ends of the earth and of the farthest seas.

PSALM 65:5

DATE:..

1 HI, GOD.

2 My day...

3 Something BIG...

Something *small*...

4

5 I'm thankful...

6 Someone needs Your help. . .

7 I'm sorry. . .

8 I need. . .

9 AMEN.

10 *You must pray at all times as the Holy Spirit leads you to pray. Pray for the things that are needed. You must watch and keep on praying. Remember to pray for all Christians.*
EPHESIANS 6:18

DATE: .... |||||||||||||||||||

1 HI, GOD.

2 My day. . .

3 Something **BIG**. . .

Something *small*. . . **4**

I'm thankful. . . **5**

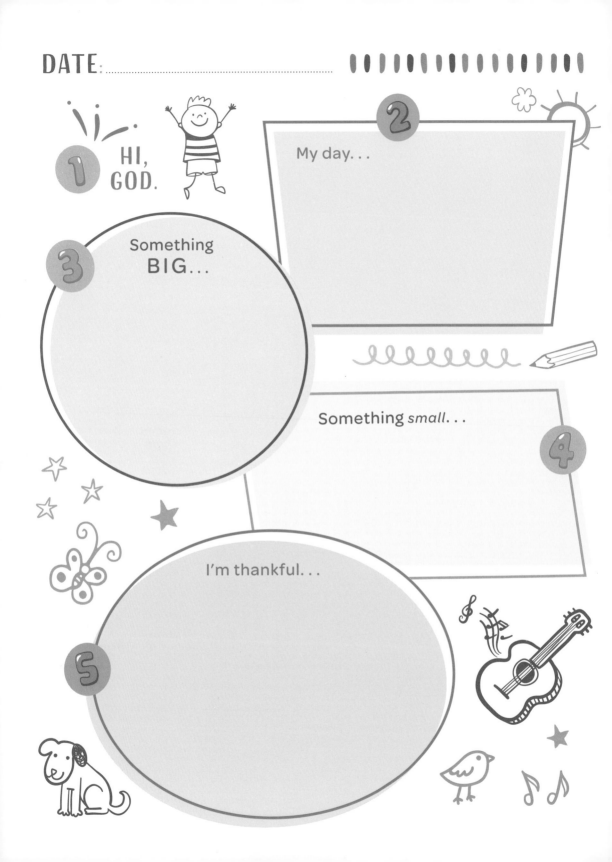

Someone needs
Your help. . .

6

I'm sorry. . .

7

8

I need. . .

9

AMEN.

10

O Lord of all, how happy is the man who trusts in You!
PSALM 84:12

DATE: ....

1 HI, GOD.

2 My day...

3 Something BIG...

Something *small*... **4**

5 I'm thankful...

6 Someone needs Your help. . .

7 I'm sorry. . .

8 I need. . .

9 AMEN.

10

I always have joy as I pray for all of you.
PHILIPPIANS 1:4

DATE:...

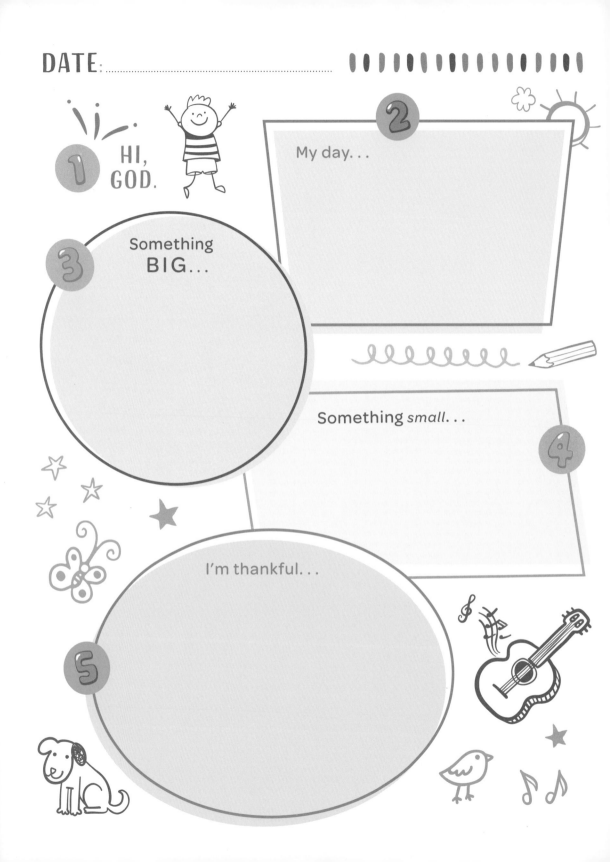

1 HI, GOD.

2 My day...

3 Something BIG...

Something *small*... **4**

5 I'm thankful...

6 Someone needs Your help. . .

7 I'm sorry. . .

8 I need. . .

9 AMEN.

10 *"When you stand to pray, if you have anything against anyone, forgive him. Then your Father in heaven will forgive your sins also."*

MARK 11:25

DATE:...

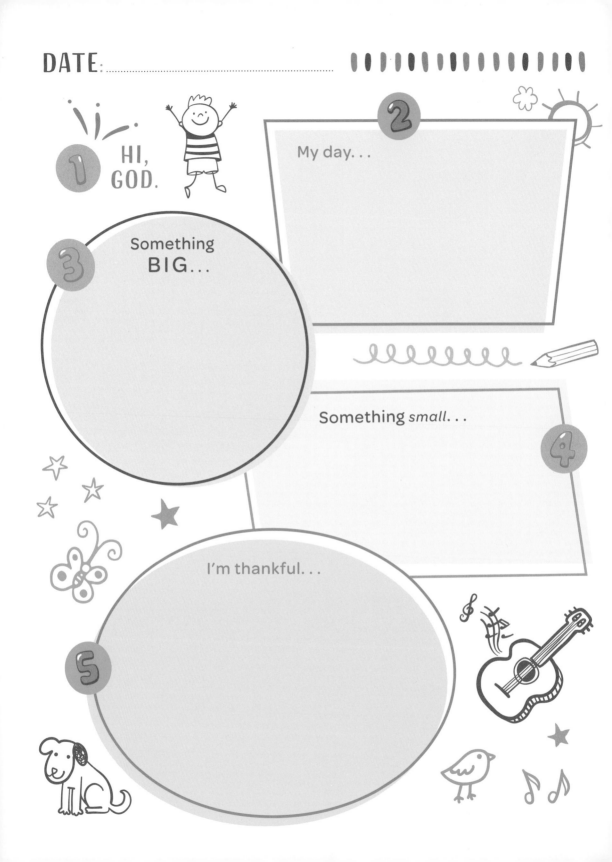

1 HI, GOD.

2 My day...

3 Something BIG...

Something *small*... **4**

I'm thankful... **5**

6 Someone needs Your help. . .

7 I'm sorry. . .

8 I need. . .

9 AMEN.

10

Do not worry. Learn to pray about everything.
Give thanks to God as you ask Him for what you need.
PHILIPPIANS 4:6

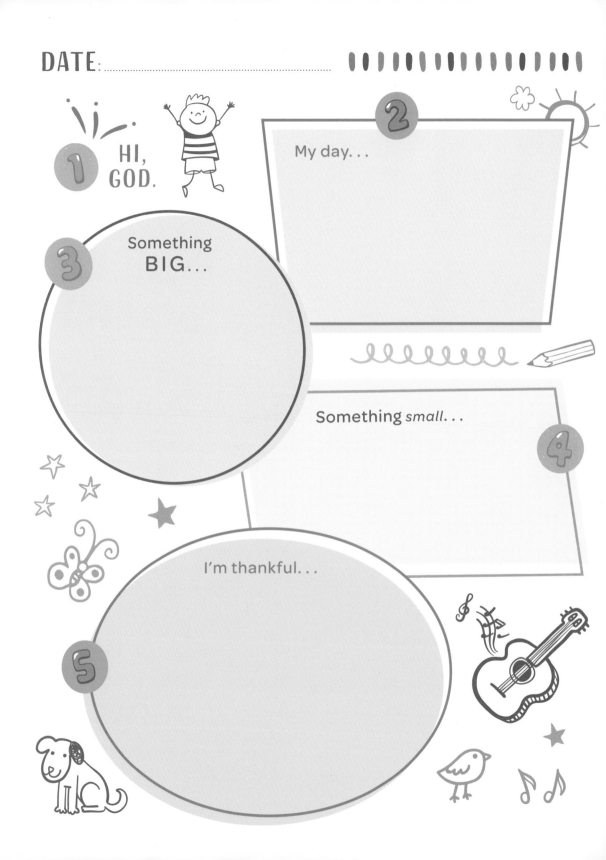

DATE:..

1 HI, GOD.

2 My day...

3 Something BIG...

Something *small*...

4

5 I'm thankful...

6 Someone needs Your help. . .

7 I'm sorry. . .

8 I need. . .

9 AMEN.

10

I pray that our faith together will help you know all the good things you have through Christ Jesus.

PHILEMON 1:6

DATE: ....

1 HI, GOD.

2 My day...

3 Something BIG...

Something *small*...

4

5 I'm thankful...

6 Someone needs Your help. . .

7 I'm sorry. . .

8 I need. . .

9 AMEN.

10 *I have never stopped praying for you since I heard about you. I ask God that you may know what He wants you to do. I ask God to fill you with the wisdom and understanding the Holy Spirit gives.*
COLOSSIANS 1:9

DATE:... ||||||||||||||||||||||

1 HI, GOD.

2 My day...

3 Something BIG...

4 Something *small*...

5 I'm thankful...

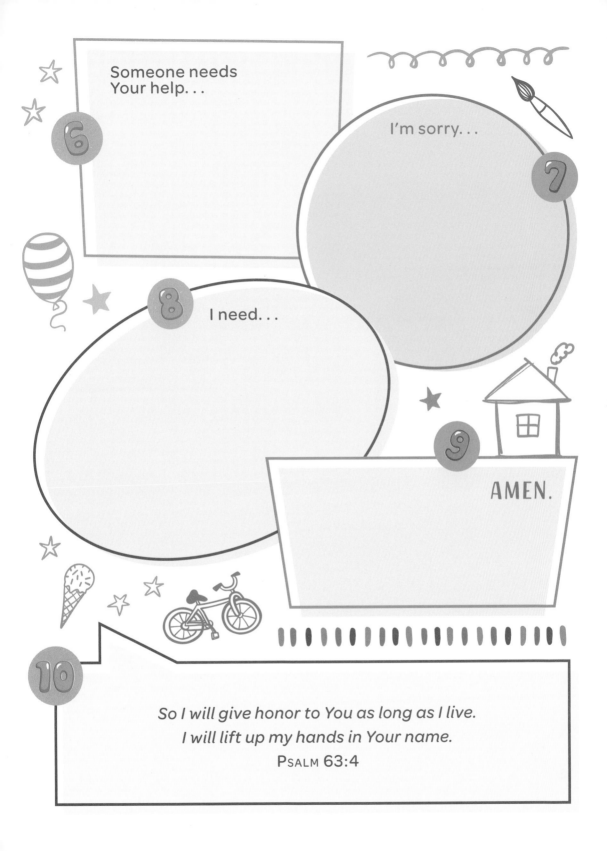

6 Someone needs Your help. . .

7 I'm sorry. . .

8 I need. . .

9 AMEN.

10

So I will give honor to You as long as I live.
I will lift up my hands in Your name.
Psalm 63:4

DATE: ....

1 HI, GOD.

2 My day...

3 Something BIG...

Something *small*...

4

5 I'm thankful...

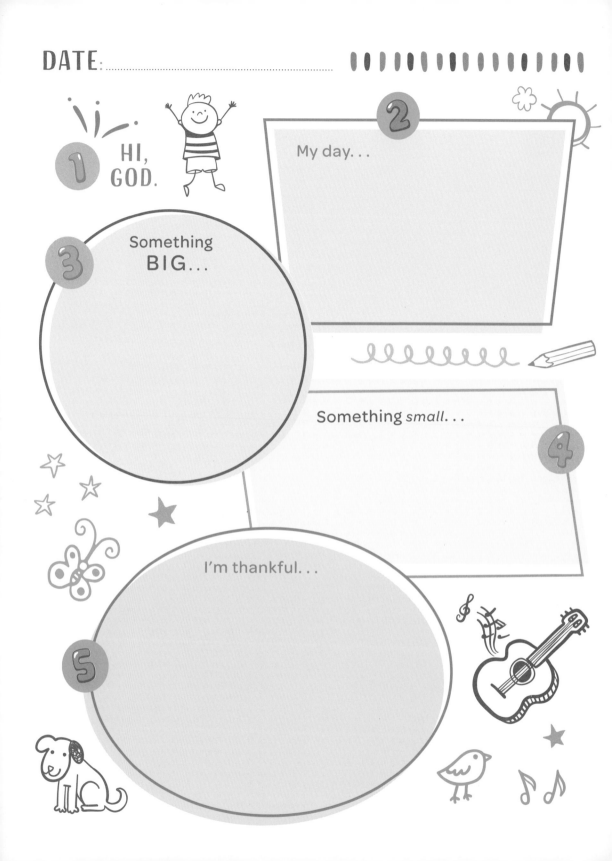

Someone needs Your help. . .

6

I'm sorry. . .

7

8

I need. . .

9

AMEN.

10

"Pray like this: 'Our Father in heaven, Your name is holy.'"
MATTHEW 6:9

DATE: ....

1 HI, GOD.

2 My day. . .

3 Something BIG...

Something *small*. . . **4**

I'm thankful. . . **5**

Someone needs Your help. . .

6

I'm sorry. . .

7

I need. . .

8

9

AMEN.

10

We always pray for you. We pray that our God will make you worth being chosen. We pray that His power will help you do the good things you want to do. We pray that your work of faith will be complete.

2 THESSALONIANS 1:11

DATE:..

1 HI, GOD.

2 My day...

3 Something BIG...

Something *small...* **4**

I'm thankful... **5**

Someone needs
Your help. . .

6

I'm sorry. . .

7

I need. . .

8

9

AMEN.

10

You answered me on the day I called.
You gave me strength in my soul.
PSALM 138:3

DATE: ....

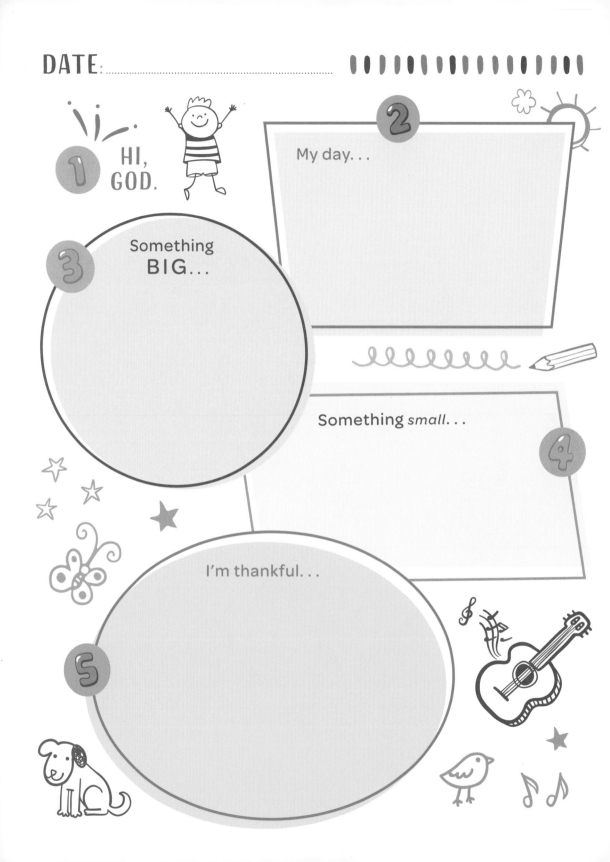

1 HI, GOD.

2 My day...

3 Something BIG...

Something *small*... **4**

5 I'm thankful...

6 Someone needs Your help. . .

7 I'm sorry. . .

8 I need. . .

9 AMEN.

10 *Trust in the Lord with all your heart, and do not trust in your own understanding.*
PROVERBS 3:5

DATE: ....

1 HI, GOD.

2 My day...

3 Something BIG...

Something *small*...

4

5 I'm thankful...

Someone needs
Your help. . .

6

I'm sorry. . .

7

I need. . .

8

9

AMEN.

10

I looked for the Lord, and He answered me.
And He took away all my fears.
Psalm 34:4

DATE:...

1 HI, GOD.

2 My day...

3 Something BIG...

Something *small*...

4

5 I'm thankful...

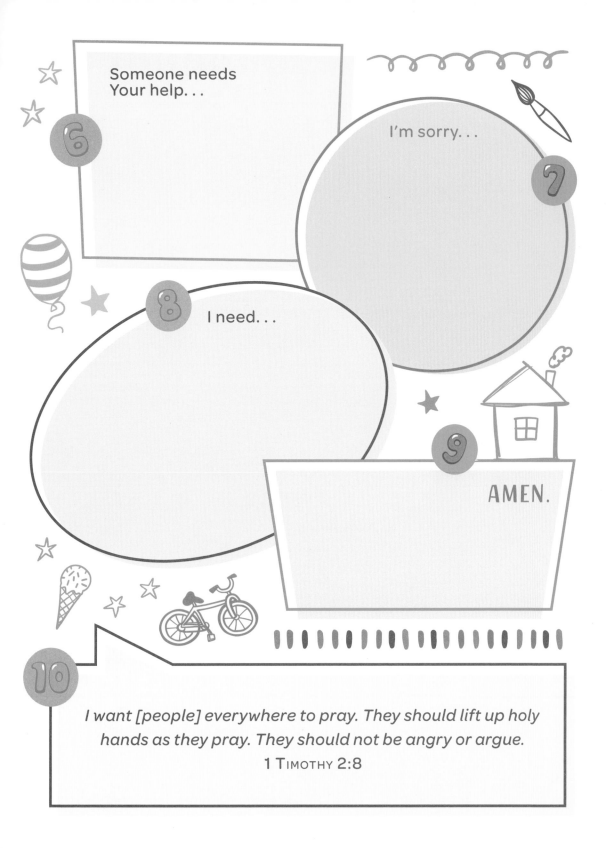

Someone needs
Your help. . .

6

I'm sorry. . .

7

I need. . .

8

AMEN.

9

10

*I want [people] everywhere to pray. They should lift up holy
hands as they pray. They should not be angry or argue.*
1 TIMOTHY 2:8

DATE:...

1 HI, GOD.

2 My day...

3 Something BIG...

Something *small*...

4

5 I'm thankful...

Someone needs Your help...

6

I'm sorry...

7

8 **I need...**

9

AMEN.

10

"I say to you, whatever you ask for when you pray, have faith that you will receive it. Then you will get it."
MARK 11:24

DATE:...

1 HI, GOD.

2 My day...

3 Something BIG...

4 Something *small*...

5 I'm thankful...

6 Someone needs Your help. . .

7 I'm sorry. . .

8 I need. . .

9 AMEN.

10 *Is anyone among you suffering? He should pray. Is anyone happy? He should sing songs of thanks to God.*
JAMES 5:13

DATE:..

1 HI, GOD.

2 My day...

3 Something BIG...

Something *small*...

4

5 I'm thankful...

Someone needs
Your help...

6

I'm sorry...

7

8

I need...

9

AMEN.

10

*I cried out to You, O Lord. I said, "You are my safe place,
my share in the land of the living."*
PSALM 142:5

DATE: ....

1 HI, GOD.

2 My day...

3 Something BIG...

Something *small*... 4

I'm thankful... 5

6 Someone needs Your help. . .

7 I'm sorry. . .

8 I need. . .

9 AMEN.

10

The Father. . .does not respect one person more than another.
1 PETER 1:17

DATE:..

1 HI, GOD.

2 My day...

3 Something BIG...

Something *small*... 4

I'm thankful... 5

6 Someone needs Your help. . .

7 I'm sorry. . .

8 I need. . .

9 AMEN.

10 *For we belong to Christ if we keep on trusting Him to the end just as we trusted Him at first.*
HEBREWS 3:14

DATE: ....

1 HI, GOD.

2 My day...

3 Something BIG...

Something *small*... 4

I'm thankful... 5

Someone needs Your help. . .

6

I'm sorry. . .

7

8 I need. . .

9 AMEN.

10

The Lord hates the gifts of the sinful,
but the prayer of the faithful is His joy.
PROVERBS 15:8

DATE: ....

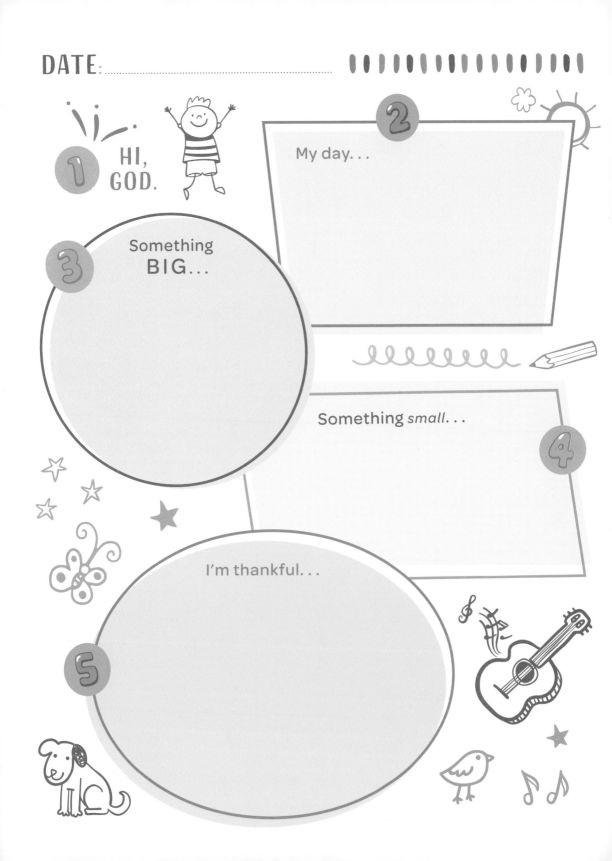

1 HI, GOD.

2 My day...

3 Something BIG...

Something *small*... **4**

5 I'm thankful...

Someone needs Your help. . .

6

I'm sorry. . .

7

I need. . .

8

9

AMEN.

10

Dear friends, you must become strong in your most holy faith. Let the Holy Spirit lead you as you pray.
JUDE 1:20

DATE: ....

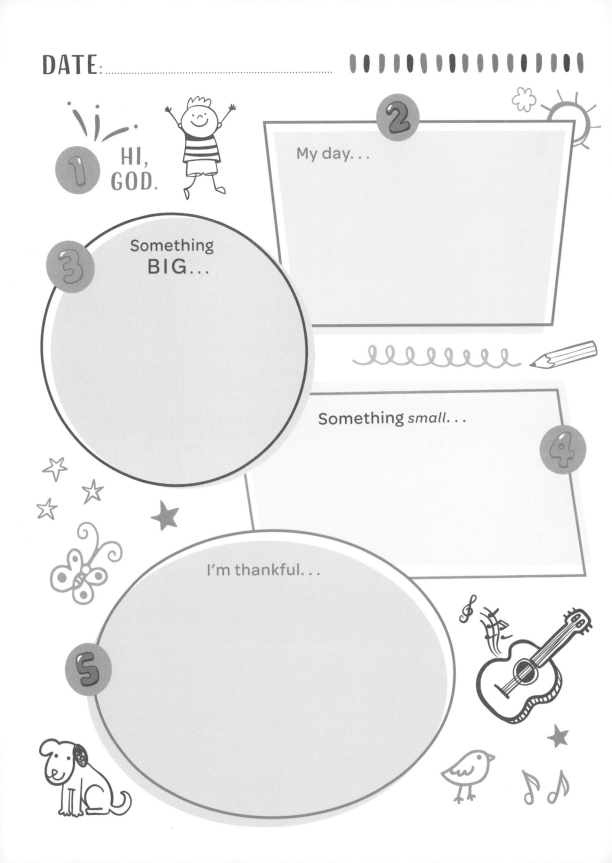

1 HI, GOD.

2 My day...

3 Something BIG...

Something *small*... **4**

5 I'm thankful...

Someone needs
Your help...

6

I'm sorry...

7

I need...

8

AMEN.

9

10

*Pray and give thanks for those who make trouble for you.
Yes, pray for them instead of talking against them.*
ROMANS **12:14**

DATE: ....

1 HI, GOD.

2 My day...

3 Something BIG...

Something *small...* **4**

I'm thankful... **5**

Someone needs
Your help...

I'm sorry...

I need...

AMEN.

The Lord has heard my cry for help.
The Lord receives my prayer.
PSALM 6:9

DATE:...................................

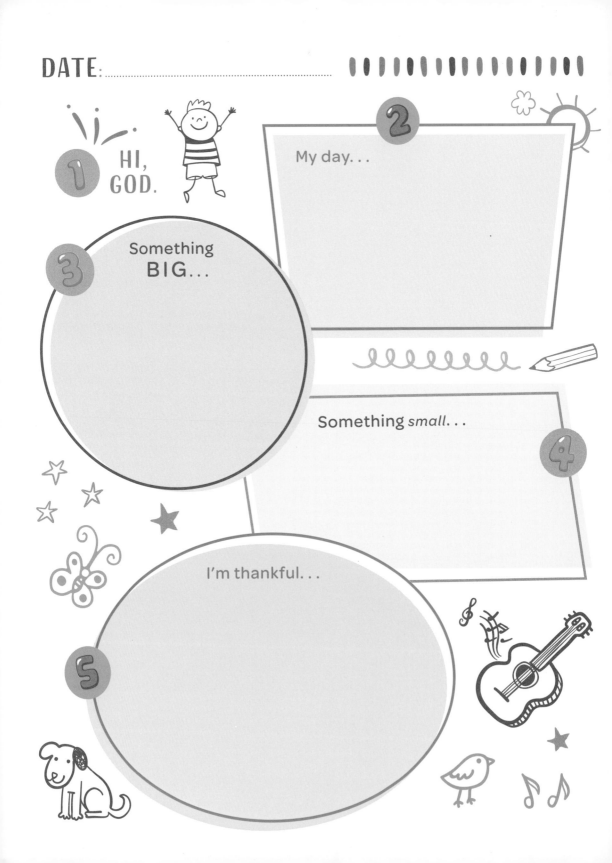

1 HI, GOD.

2 My day...

3 Something BIG...

Something small...

4

I'm thankful...

5

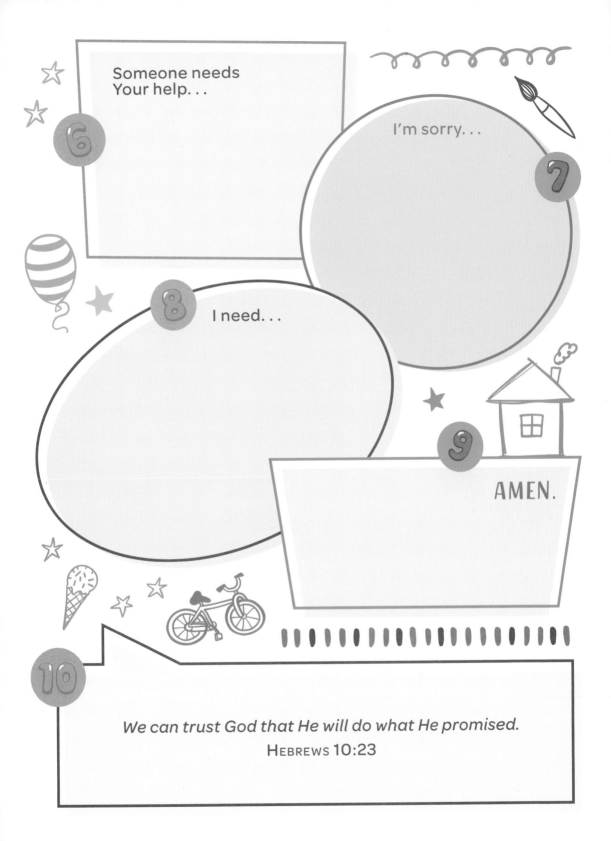

Someone needs
Your help...

6

I'm sorry...

7

I need...

8

9

AMEN.

10

We can trust God that He will do what He promised.
HEBREWS 10:23

DATE: ....

1 HI, GOD.

2 My day...

3 Something BIG...

Something *small*...

4

5 I'm thankful...

6 Someone needs Your help...

7 I'm sorry...

8 I need...

9 AMEN.

10

I am always with You. You hold me by my right hand.
Psalm 73:23

DATE: ....

1 HI, GOD.

2 My day...

3 Something BIG...

Something *small*...

4

5 I'm thankful...

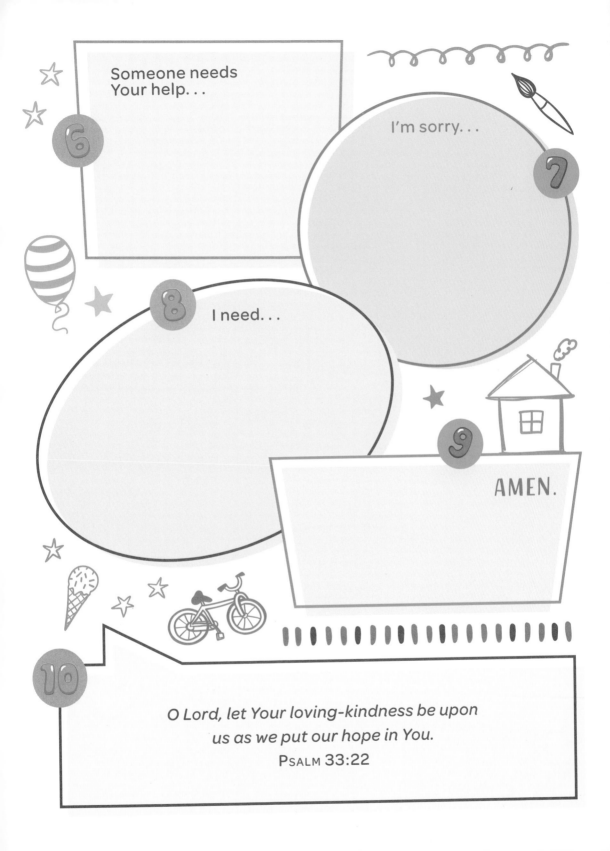

6 Someone needs Your help. . .

7 I'm sorry. . .

8 I need. . .

9 AMEN.

10 *O Lord, let Your loving-kindness be upon us as we put our hope in You.*
PSALM 33:22

DATE: ....

1 HI, GOD.

2 My day...

3 Something BIG...

Something *small*...

4

5 I'm thankful...

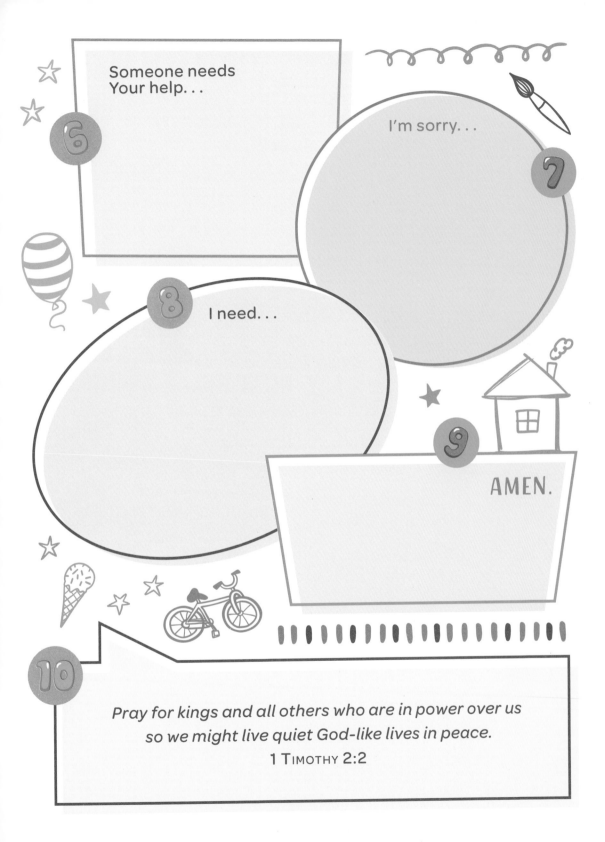

Someone needs
Your help. . .

6

I'm sorry. . .

7

8

I need. . .

9

AMEN.

10

Pray for kings and all others who are in power over us
so we might live quiet God-like lives in peace.
1 TIMOTHY 2:2

DATE:...

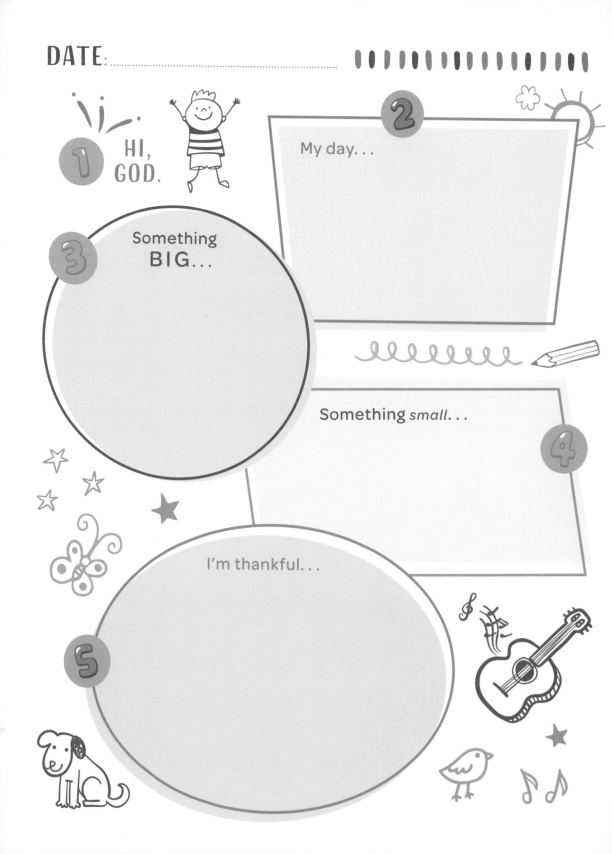

1 HI, GOD.

2 My day...

3 Something BIG...

Something *small*...

4

I'm thankful...

5

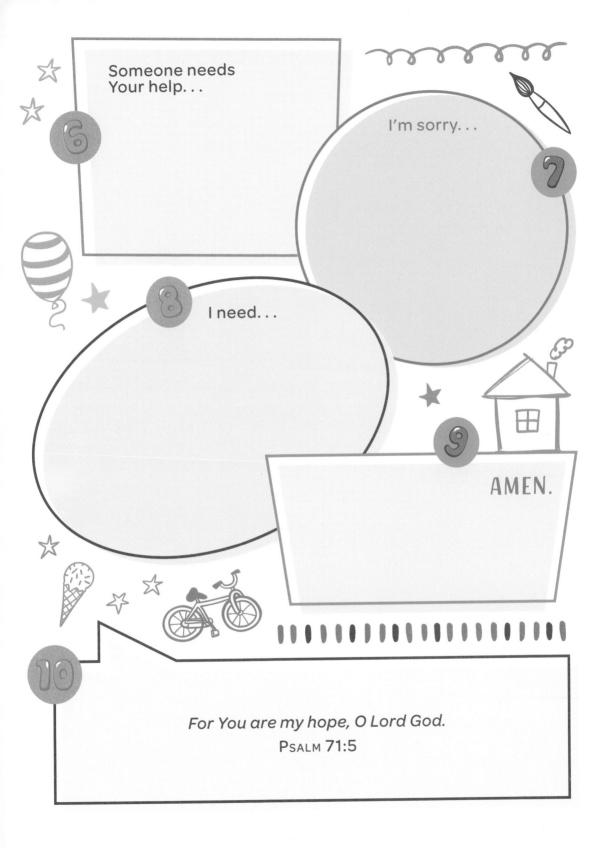

6 Someone needs Your help. . .

7 I'm sorry. . .

8 I need. . .

9 AMEN.

10 *For You are my hope, O Lord God.*
PSALM 71:5

DATE: ....

1 HI, GOD.

2 My day...

3 Something BIG...

Something *small*... **4**

I'm thankful... **5**

Someone needs Your help. . .

6

I'm sorry. . .

7

8 **I need. . .**

9 AMEN.

10

"The Lord watches over those who are right with Him. He hears their prayers."
1 PETER 3:12

DATE:...

1 HI, GOD.

2 My day...

3 Something BIG...

Something *small*... 4

5 I'm thankful...

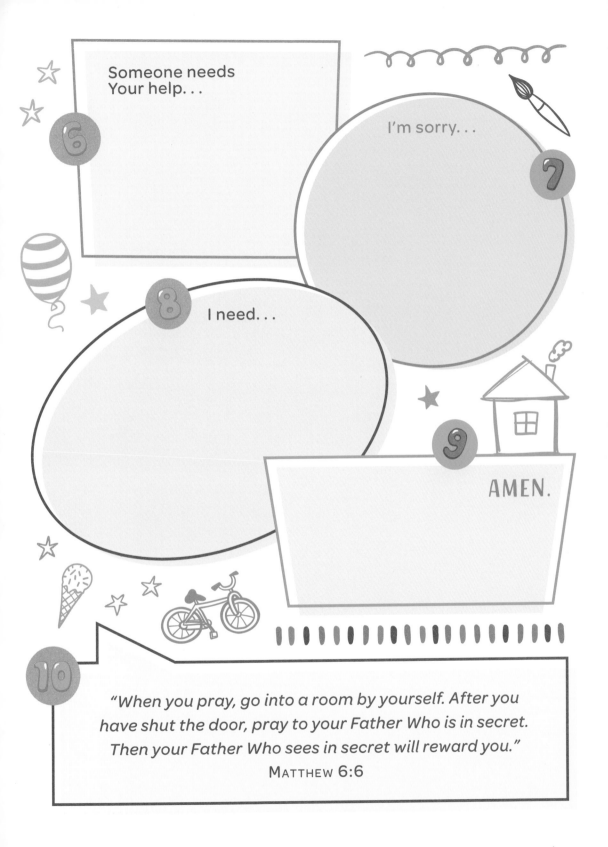

6 Someone needs Your help. . .

7 I'm sorry. . .

8 I need. . .

9 AMEN.

10 *"When you pray, go into a room by yourself. After you have shut the door, pray to your Father Who is in secret. Then your Father Who sees in secret will reward you."*
MATTHEW 6:6

DATE: ....

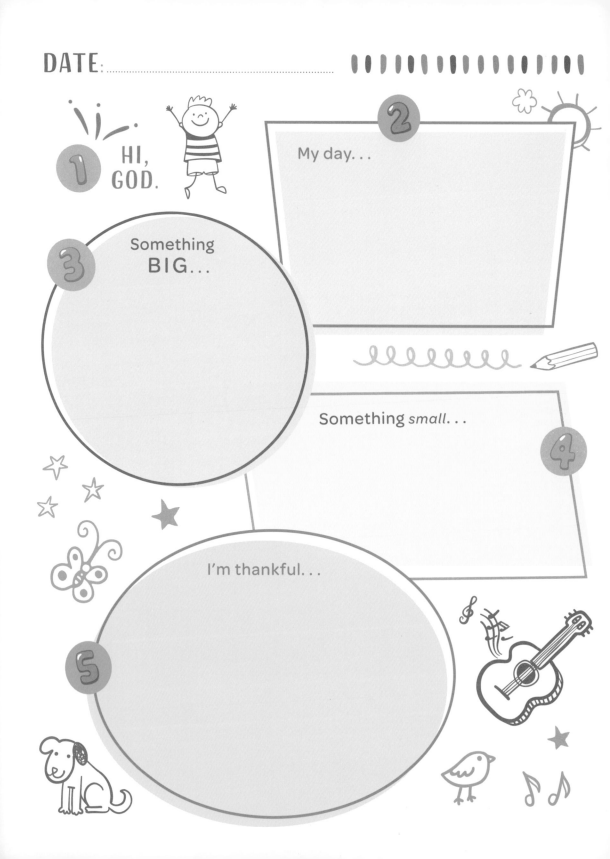

1 HI, GOD.

2 My day...

3 Something BIG...

4 Something *small*...

5 I'm thankful...

6 Someone needs Your help. . .

7 I'm sorry. . .

8 I need. . .

9 AMEN.

10

Keep awake so you can pray.
1 PETER 4:7

DATE:..

1 HI, GOD.

2 My day...

3 Something BIG...

Something *small*... **4**

I'm thankful... **5**

6 Someone needs Your help. . .

7 I'm sorry. . .

8 I need. . .

9 AMEN.

10 *Praise the Lord! Praise the Lord, O my soul! I will praise the Lord as long as I live. I will sing praises to my God as long as I live.*
PSALM 146:1–2

DATE: .... |||||||||||||||||||||

1 HI, GOD.

2 My day...

3 Something BIG...

Something *small*... **4**

5 I'm thankful...

6 Someone needs Your help...

7 I'm sorry...

8 I need...

9 AMEN.

10

When my worry is great within me,
Your comfort brings joy to my soul.
PSALM 94:19

DATE: ....

1 HI, GOD.

2 My day. . .

3 Something BIG. . .

Something *small*. . . 4

5 I'm thankful. . .

6 Someone needs Your help. . .

7 I'm sorry. . .

8 I need. . .

9 AMEN.

10 *I wait for the Lord. My soul waits and I hope in His Word.*
PSALM 130:5

DATE: ....

1 HI, GOD.

2 My day...

3 Something BIG...

Something *small*...

4

I'm thankful...

5

6 Someone needs Your help. . .

7 I'm sorry. . .

8 I need. . .

9 AMEN.

10 "No one who puts his trust in Christ
will ever be put to shame."
Romans 10:11

DATE: ....

1. HI, GOD.

2. My day...

3. Something **BIG**...

Something *small*...

4.

5. I'm thankful...

6 Someone needs Your help...

7 I'm sorry...

8 I need...

9 AMEN.

10

The hope of those who are right with God is joy.
PROVERBS 10:28

DATE: .... |||||||||||||||||||||||

1 HI, GOD.

2 My day...

3 Something BIG...

Something *small*... **4**

5 I'm thankful...

6 Someone needs Your help. . .

7 I'm sorry. . .

8 I need. . .

9 AMEN.

10 *God knows how I work for Him. He knows how I preach with all my heart the Good News about His Son. He knows how I always pray for you.*

ROMANS 1:9

DATE: ....

1 HI, GOD.

2 My day...

3 Something **BIG**...

Something *small*...

4

5 I'm thankful...

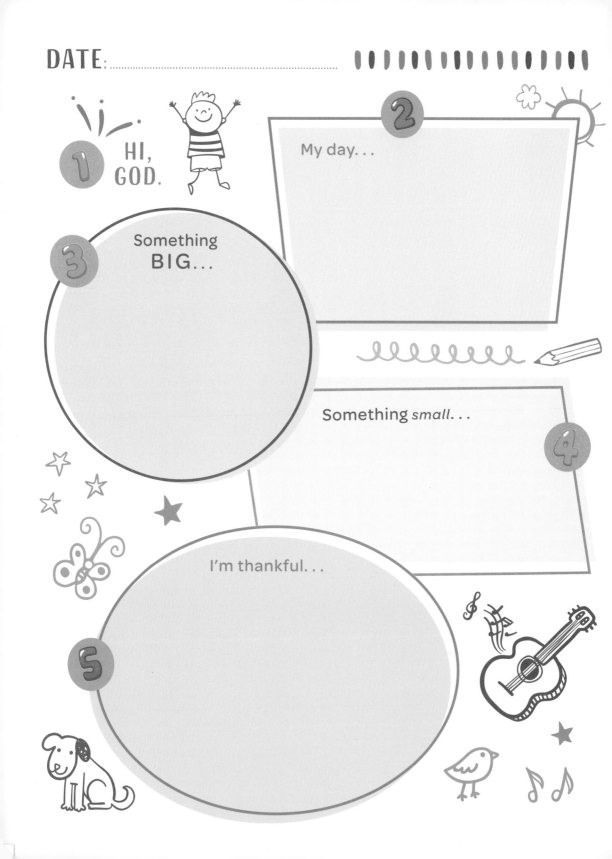

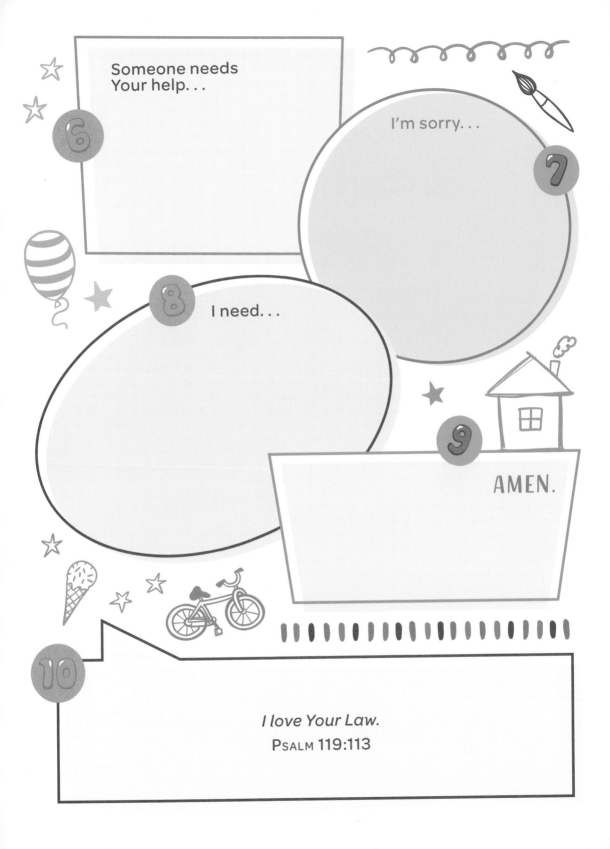

Someone needs
Your help...

6

I'm sorry...

7

8

I need...

9

AMEN.

10

I love Your Law.
PSALM 119:113

DATE: _____

1 HI, GOD.

2 My day...

3 Something BIG...

Something *small*...

4

5 I'm thankful...

Someone needs Your help. . .

6

I'm sorry. . .

7

8

I need. . .

9

AMEN.

10

Rest in the Lord and be willing to wait for Him.
PSALM 37:7

DATE:_____

1. HI, GOD.

2. My day...

3. Something BIG...

4. Something small...

5. I'm thankful...

6 Someone needs Your help. . .

7 I'm sorry. . .

8 I need. . .

9 AMEN.

10 *I will give thanks to You, for You have answered me. And You are the One Who saves me.*
PSALM 118:21

DATE:

1 HI, GOD.

2 My day...

3 Something BIG...

Something *small*... **4**

5 I'm thankful...

6 Someone needs Your help...

7 I'm sorry...

8 I need...

9 AMEN.

10 *I pray that you will know about the hope given by God's call. I pray that you will see how great the things are that He has promised to those who belong to Him.*

EPHESIANS 1:18

DATE: .... |||||||||||||||||||||

1 HI, GOD.

2 My day...

3 Something BIG...

Something *small*... **4**

I'm thankful... **5**

6 Someone needs Your help...

7 I'm sorry...

8 I need...

9 AMEN.

10

Answer me when I call, O my God Who is right and good!
PSALM 4:1

DATE:

1 HI, GOD.

2 My day...

3 Something BIG...

Something *small*...

4

5 I'm thankful...

6 Someone needs Your help. . .

7 I'm sorry. . .

8 I need. . .

9 AMEN.

10 *I thank God for you whenever I think of you.*
PHILIPPIANS 1:3

DATE: ....

1 HI, GOD.

2 My day...

3 Something BIG...

Something *small*... **4**

I'm thankful... **5**

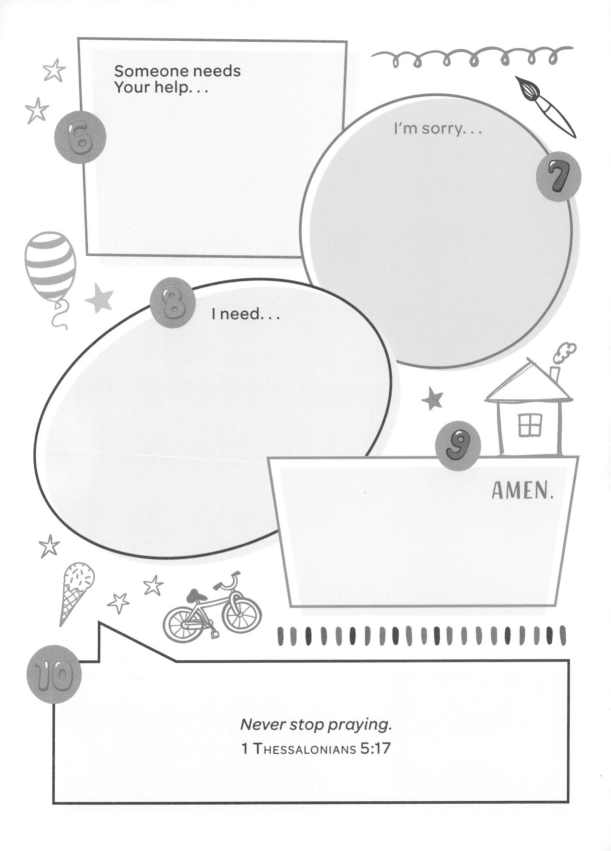

6 Someone needs Your help...

7 I'm sorry...

8 I need...

9 AMEN.

10 *Never stop praying.*
1 THESSALONIANS 5:17

Interactive Journal Encourages Kids to Live Out Their Faith in Real Life!

Read It! Pray It! Write It! Draw It! Do It!

This fun, interactive journal for kids will help them grow in their faith. With Bible-related reading, praying, writing, drawing, and doing activities, the kids in your life will enjoy the varied prompts. Touching on topics that will enhance a child's faith, like praying, making decisions, waiting, forgiving, obeying, being kind, being more like Jesus, loving others, and more, kids will be encouraged to read a scripture passage (a key Bible passage is included), pray about it (a prayer starter is included), journal their own thoughts and feelings (a journal prompt is included), and draw a related picture (a drawing prompt is included). Each topically arranged section wraps up with a related "doing" activity as well—encouraging kids to live out their faith in real life!

Paperback / 978-1-68322-865-3 / $12.99